Tabletop Aquaponics For Beginners!

I0421136

Aquaponics

A Step By Step Aquaponics Gardening Guide For Growing Vegetables And Raising Fish In Your Home Or Backyard!

David Wright

STOP!!! Before you read any further....Would you like to know the secrets of Anti - Aging?

If your answer is yes, then you are not alone. Thousands of people are looking for the secret to reducing wrinkles, looking younger, and maintaining a youthful appearance.

If you have been searching for these answers without much luck, you are in the right place!

Not only will you gain incredible insight in this book, but because I want to make sure to give you as much value as possible, right now for a limited time you can get full **100% FREE access to a VIP bonus EBook** entitled **Anti - Aging Made Easy!**

Legal Notice

Disclaimer Notice

Table Of Contents

Introduction

Chapter 1: An Introduction To Aquaponics Gardening

Chapter 2: Aquaponics Gardening Benefits

Chapter 3: Step-By-Step Guide For Starting Aquaponics Gardening

Chapter 4: Start Up Costs Of Aquaponics Gardening

Chapter 5: Seeds To Use For Aquaponics Garden

Chapter 6: Best Plants To Use For Your Aquaponics Garden

Chapter 7: Best Fish To Use In Your Aquaponics Garden

Chapter 8: Aquaponics vs. Hydroponics

Chapter 9: Tips And Tricks For A Successful Aquaponics Garden

Chapter 10: Caring Tips For Your Fish And Plants

Chapter 11: Shopping List For Starting Your Aquaponics Garden

Conclusion

Preview Of: "Fly Fishing: A Fly Fishing Guide To Catching Trout Using Grandfather's Success Secrets For Fly Fishing!"

Free Bonus Offer

Introduction

I want to thank you and congratulate you for purchasing the book, *"Tabletop Aquaponics For Beginners: Aquaponics-A Step By Step Aquaponics Gardening Guide For Growing Vegetables And Raising Fish In Your Home Or Backyard"*.

This "Aquaponics" book contains proven steps and strategies on how to plan, set up and maintain an aquaponics system right in your own home or backyard. The system may look a bit intimidating, but this book will walk you through every step.

In this book, you will learn the following:

- What aquaponics is all about

- What types of systems can be used

- What are the basic units

- What are the benefits

- How to set up your own system

- How to choose fishes and plants

- Success tips

And so much more.

Read this book and learn everything there is to know about aquaponics.

Thanks again for purchasing this book, I hope you enjoy it!

Chapter 1: An Introduction To Aquaponics Gardening

Aquaponics gardening is growing plants and raising fish at the same time, in a well-controlled environment. This setup takes advantage of the symbiotic relationship between fishes and plants. The waste products from the fish provide nutrients for the plants. On the other hand, the plants keep the water clean and well-oxygenated, giving the fish the perfect living habitat.

Basic Components

There are 2 major parts of a typical aquaponics setup: the aquaculture portion, where you will be raising the fish or other aquatic animals such as shrimp and crayfish, and the hydroponics section, where the plants are grown.

The entire system is closed. That is, the water is circulated and recirculated between the aquaculture and hydroponics parts. Effluents or wastes accumulate in the aquatic tank, which comes from left over feed and animal waste. This build up creates a toxic environment for the aquatic animals. This is where the hydroponics setup comes in handy. The "dirty" water is brought up to the hydroponics setup. The effluents are toxic to the animals, but are much needed nutrients for the plants.

All aquaponics systems are composed of these 2 main parts, but are often grouped further into subsystems. These subsystems or components function for solid waste removal, maintain water oxygenation or for neutralizing pH. Typically, components are the following:

- Rearing tank

  The rearing tank is any large container where the fish and other aquatic animals will live.

- Settling basin

  This unit is responsible for catching any leftover feed and any detached biofilm. It is also used as a receptacle where fine particulates are allowed to settle.

- Biofilter

  This component holds the bacteria responsible for the nitrification process. The biofilter unit is where bacteria convert the ammonia from the fish wastes into nitrates that the plants use for nourishment.

- Hydroponics subsystem

  This is where the plants are. The main function of the hydroponics subsystem is to act as a filtering system that removes nitrates from the water and returns the clean and fresh water back into the rest of the system.

- Sump

  This is the lowest point of the entire aquaponics system. Water flows into the sump from the hydroponics, already clean. It is then pumped out and brought back into the rearing tank.

Chapter 2: Aquaponics Gardening Benefits

Aquaponics gardening is a sustainable type of raising food like plants and fishes.

Environmentally Friendly

The way aquaponics gardens works, they are able to recycle materials within their system. In essence, the natural wastes from the fishes are possible water pollutants. But because of the presence of microbes and plants, the water will remain clear and habitable for the fishes and other aquatic life. The plants filter the water, removing the waste and use them as food. The clean water is returned back into the garden. This essentially keeps the garden clean and fresh at all times.

Because of this basic setup, an aquaponics system does not require fertilizers or any chemicals. Furthermore, the entire system does not cause pollution to the environment and the produce is free from any harmful toxins and chemical residues.

Water Conservation

At first glance, an aquaponics system looks as if it uses too much water, maybe because of the large tanks that are used. The system actually uses much less water compared to conventional farming methods. Water from the tanks is continuously recycled. Waste-laden water from the fish tanks are brought o the plant bins for filtering, then returned clean and fresh for the fish. So basically, water placed at setup is the same water used for the rest of the operation. From time to time, you will need to add more water to account for evaporation, but the additions are considerably minimal and done much less frequently. More water is conserved if water used is from collected rain water. This way, the system does not contribute to water consumption and wastage problem.

Because of this, the aquaponics system can be used even in environments that are experiencing droughts. It is more like having a small oasis in the middle of a desert. All the water in the system is efficiently used and reused, reducing the need for huge water inputs on a regular basis.

More Yields

Aquaponics gardeners report higher yields in less time compared to conventional gardening methods. Vegetables grown in aquaponics systems tend to grow larger, about 3 to 4 times denser than average. Plants grow and bear fruit faster than average, without using up all the nutrients in the system. This is because there is a steady supply of nutrients from the waste conversion happening in the fish waste and the microbes. In comparison, plants growing in the soil deplete the nutrients with each planting season. That is why most farmers are forced to augment soil nutrients with chemicals and fertilizers. Adding mulch can only add very small amounts of nutrients that are immediately used up. Another alternative is to rest the soil (no planting) for at least a season to allow the soil to recover.

Space Saver

Farmlands need to be expansive in order to generate a considerable yield. This is not just any kind of land. The soil has to be fertile. There has to be a good and steady access to water, good drainage system and ample sunlight, among other considerations.

These are not factors when using aquaponics. The system does not need soil.

100% Chemical Free

The most attractive benefit is most probably its 100% organic growing methods. Even the fish can be certified organically raised. First, pesticides, insecticides and other chemicals commonly used on plants are highly discouraged. These chemicals are potentially harmful to the fishes. Even the "organic pesticides" can harm the fishes. Hence, there is no cheating when it comes to aquaponics.

Weed- and Pest-Free

Weeding is a backbreaking task necessary in soil cultivation. Pests are also a problem with soil gardening. Hand-picking worms and bugs is also too much work. Other non-chemical solutions to weed and pest problems can only do so much. For those who do not have the time or energy, herbicides, pesticides, insecticides and other chemicals are applied to kill the weeds and pests. These products leave harmful residue on the plants and pollute the soil.

With the aquaponics system, tilling, compost shredding, fertilizing, chemical sprays and all the other hard work are no longer required. No bending down, either. All work is done standing up. There is no weeding needed. Work needed with aquaponics s as simple as fixing the electricity, giving fish food, adding seeds and fixing the potting media.

Chapter 3: Step-By-Step Guide For Starting Aquaponics Gardening

Starting an aquaponics garden is pretty easy. It can be a DIY project or professional help can be called in. It can be more adventurous and more rewarding when setting it up on your own.

Guide to Setting Up Aquaponics System

1. Picking the site.

   This is the most important step that any aquaponics grower should do first. This will determine what type of system to setup and the sizes of the equipments to be used. At some level, the location will also determine what types of fish and plants can be raised and grown. Also, make sure that the site does not see too much human traffic. Also, make sure that the site is not directly exposed to sunlight.

2. Power

   Make sure that the setup has a good, safe and secure access to a power supply. Electricity is important in running the air and water pumps. If you're planning for an outdoor setup, electrical equipment should be weatherproof. To make your hydroponics rig truly "green" you might want to consider using solar panels as a power source.

3. Setting up the Plant Bin

   The plant bin or tub (also called as the growing tub or bin) is where the plants will be grown. It is built above the fish tank so that the water from this bin will flow freely into the fish bin. Some people just poke a hole at the bottom of the growing bin to allow water to trickle down into the fish tank. Some opt to use hoses for this goal.

4. Connecting the hoses.

   The hoses are connected from the fish tank to the plant bin. Water from the fishes will be drawn up to water the plants via hoses.

5. Adding water.

   Test the system by adding purified water. See if the water is flowing smoothly and continuously. Once the plants start growing, expect the water flow to slow down.

6. Test the timer.

   The water and air pumps do not have to run continuously, which is why most setups have timers. Set up the timer to the recommended on/off cycles. Test to make sure it turns off and on in the right intervals.

7. Setting up the fish tank.

   After the hoses, timers and other equipments are put in place, it is now time to add the living things. Add the fishes in their designated tanks. Cycle the fish tank to make sure that the levels of ammonia are low and the nitrate-nitrite are maintained at required levels. Cycling should occur naturally but test the waters from time to time just to make sure everything is working well. This is also an important step before the plants are added. This is to make sure that there is adequate bacterial population available to convert fish waste into plant food. Otherwise, there won't be enough food when the plants are placed in the system.

8. Adding the plants.

   Place the growing media in the growing bins. Then, add the plants.

9. Tank Maintenance

   Once the aquaponics garden is set up, there is very little to do. What is needed is to maintain that the system is working as it should. Monitor the levels of ammonia, nitrates and nitrites, just to make sure everything is working well. Changing the water won't be necessary because the plants work as the natural filtering system. Feed the fish with the recommended food specific for their species.

Types of Aquaponics System

There are 3 main types of system set up in aquaponics. The types include media filled beds, nutrient film technique and deep water culture.

Media Filled Beds

This is the most common and simplest aquaponics system. Containers are filled with rock media and expanded clay, or something similar. The fish tank is filled water and is pumped into the media-filled beds, where the plants are grown. There are 2 ways to run a media filled bed system. One, water is in continuous flow over the rock media. Another way is by flooding. This can be carried out through a cycle of flooding and draining or ebb and flow cycle of the grow beds.

Nutrient Film Technique (NFT)

This is more commonly used in hydroponics but works well in aquaponics too. With this system, water rich in nutrients are pumped downwards into gutters in very thin films. The plants are placed in plastic cups with their roots having direct access to the nutrient-rich waters. Certain plants, such as leafy greens grow well in this system. Plants with larger and wider root systems won't thrive well in this system.

Deep Water System

This is basically placing plants in floating systems with the roots hanging down straight into the water.

Chapter 4: Start Up Costs Of Aquaponics Gardening

Small home or backyard aquaponics systems are generally not the best type of financial investment. Because of the limited space, yield is mostly enough for home use. There isn't enough harvest to sell in local markets. The best benefit will be having a supply of the best tasting, most nutritious and freshest food all year long. Larger aquaponics systems do provide a good return of investment, as the grower continuously harvests and sells the produce.

Stand-alone and Climatically-Adapted Aquaponics Setup

This type of setup is most common in areas with changing climates such as in the temperate regions. The system has to be kept at constant temperatures to ensure plant and fish survival during the changing seasons.

A 10 feet by 16 feet greenhouse structure that contains 1 grow tray that measures 12 feet in length and 5 feet in width. This size provides 60 square feet of growing tray space. The yield is approximately enough to feed 2 people in a year. An initial investment will cost around US$4,800.

A structure with dimensions of 18 feet by 32 feet can comfortably support 2 grow trays measuring 6 feet by 28 feet. The approximate growing tray space is 336 square feet, producing enough food for approximately 13 people in a year. An initial investment for this space is US$8,100.

These are just approximations and largely based on a simple structural design. It does not include landscaping and other aesthetic materials.

Additional cost is needed if installing equipment for temperature regulation. Materials to help protect the plants and fishes from extreme effects of cold, heat and sun also adds to the cost.

Other things that can add to the abovementioned estimated cost are grow lights, wet walls, fans and ventilation systems. Grow lights are recommended for areas that receive limited sunlight. It is also a good addition during the winter months so that there is continuous and good growth rates for plants such as tomatoes and flowering plants. In areas with hot climates or during the summer months, a good ventilation and cooling system is recommended to prevent dehydrating the plants and fish kills. Too hot environmental conditions can affect the oxygen levels of the water, which can kill the fishes. Plants not adapted to extreme hot conditions can scorch and wither. To prevent problems like these, additional funds are needed for installation of cooling and ventilation.

Other added costs would also come from the seeds, plants, fish, fish food, water and electricity.

With the basic estimated cost, let us take a look at the economies of scale. That is, how much is spent for each person benefitting from the aquaponics system. The smaller aquaponics system costs US$4,800 supporting two full grown people in a year. Therefore, in order to support each person, the investment is at US$2,400 for each person supported. Now let us take a look at the larger unit. This unit costs more than the smaller one, at US$8,100. The system is able to support 13 grown people in a year. That would be spending only US$623 for each person. Thus, a larger aquaponics system may cost more but on the economies of scale, is much cheaper.

Therefore, a larger unit is invariably cheaper in the long run. It gives better investment returns.

Chapter 5: Seeds To Use For Aquaponics Garden

The plants in the aquaponics system can come from seeds instead of buying full-grown plants. Starting from seeds requires knowledge of how to grow the seeds and what media are best suited for them.

Growing Seeds

There are basically 3 methods of growing plants from seeds. These are broadcasting, germinating through wet paper towels and starting seeds with media.

Broadcasting

This is the easiest way of growing from seeds. It also requires the least from the grower in terms or work and materials. Broadcasting can be done in both soil and soil-less environments. This method simply means the grower broadcasts or tosses the seeds over a growing surface. The seed should be scattered evenly, without any seeds lying on top of each other.

This method is good for carrots and lettuce seeds. It can also work well with other small seeds typically sowed in early spring and are well adapted to very wet growing conditions.

Wet Paper Towel Germination

This method works well with seeds larger than lettuce seeds, and able to germinate fast such as seeds of peas, cucumbers, beans and melons. These seeds often do not do well when sowed directly into grow beds.

To use this method, you will need a wet (but not dripping wet) paper towel. The seeds are arranged in a single layer, and then sealed in a large resealable bag. Check each day for any sprouts. Also, check that the paper towel to make sure it remains wet all throughout the germination period. Once the roots have grown to a decent length of at least 1 inch, remove them from the paper towel. Gently place the sprouted seedlings into the growing media.

Make sure that the roots will get wet adequately during the flood cycles.

Media

Seeds can also be germinated using growing media. This is most applicable for seeds that are much harder to germinate, like chard and spinach. Seeds that require more attention during the germination period such as peppers and tomatoes will also do well starting on growing media.

Media that can be used include rockwool and peat sponges.

- Rockwool

  Rockwool is the default starting media for starting seeds in hydroponics. This media is completely inert, which promotes a sterile environment for seedling starting. There is no chance that the conditions will not support insects or fungus. The disadvantage is that rockwool needs to have its pH kept in balance. It is also made from spun rock material, which can be difficult to work with.

- Peat Sponge

  This media is based on biological materials such as latex and peat. There is no need to monitor and adjust pH. The materials are biodegradable, which allow good seed growth and are great to work with.

  The disadvantage is that this media is a good place for fungal gnats. These can also get pricey.

Chapter 6: Best Plants To Use For Your Aquaponics Garden

Generally, leafy vegetables thrive well in hydroponic subsystems of an aquaponics garden. Some growers even report harvesting leafy vegetables with huge leaves, several times broader than average. Some vegetables have leaves that can cover an entire grown person. The continuous supply of nutrient-rich water supports faster and larger leaf growths.

Some choose their plants according to their profitability. The best ones would include the following:

- Lettuce
- Chinese cabbage
- Tomatoes
- Bell peppers
- Basil
- Cantaloupe
- Okra
- Roses
- Swiss chard
- Mint
- Watercress
- Chives
- Basil
- Kale
- Arugula

Some plants are suited for aquaponics but have higher nutritional demands. These plants are suitable only when the aquaponics system is already well established, and the fish tank heavily stocked. Plants like:

- Cabbage
- Broccoli
- Cucumbers
- Peas
- Squash
- Beans
- Cauliflower
- Tomatoes
- Peppers

How to Decide What to Grow and When

Take notice of what type of root system of the plants considered for the system. Plants that have no established root structures would require floating beds. Leafy greens and herbs are ideally grown in a floating beds, raft-style. Root vegetables require wicking beds for good growth. Plants with other root systems generally grow well in media beds. Examples include peppers, tomatoes, beans and other multiple yield plants.

Even with aquaponics, growers need to consider the general climate in the area and if the plants are suited for it. This is especially important if the aquaponics system is placed outdoors. If indoors or in a greenhouse, a wide range of vegetables can be grown.

Chapter 7: Best Fish To Use In Your Aquaponics Garden

Fishes are important factors in a sustainable aquaponics garden. The most common ones are freshwater fishes. Sometimes, prawns and crayfish can also be raised.

The most popular fish raised through aquaponics is tilapia. Other popular fishes are Murray cod, silver perch, barramundi, tandanus catfish or eel-tailed catfish and jade perch.

In temperate climates, maintaining water temperatures are often the least priority. If adding fishes to these gardens, the best ones that can withstand the climate are catfish and bluegill. If raising fishes not for food purposes, goldfish and koi are good choices.

Catfish

Catfishes grow fast and require very little maintenance. They are one of the easiest fishes to raise. The only disadvantage is the supply. Availability of the fingerlings is for a limited time only, May to July of each year. Because of this, all fingerlings purchased are of the same age, which means harvesting an entire batch all at the same time. It is difficult to stagger harvest in an attempt to keep a continuous supply.

Koi

These are also easy to raise but are not edible. They only make good pets. Fingerlings are available any time of the year. They also grow fast. Koi are good to include in an aquaponics system because they produce large amounts of wastes.

Goldfish

These are also excellent fishes to add to the aquaponics garden. Add a gallon of water for every 5 to 10 goldfish. They grow very slowly and not too large. Like koi, their waste is the only thing that the system can get from them. Also, growers may need to take a few fishes out of the tank from time to time to avoid overcrowding. Goldfish relatively reproduce fast. One natural way to control their population is to add natural predators like catfish, perch or bass.

Salmon and Trout

These are only good for aquaponics systems in colder climates. While these fishes fetch a good price and has a good market demand, raising them requires quite a lot of work. Fingerlings are only available on certain times of the year, much like the catfish problem. Also, the system has to have a special arrangement for double heat exchange. Water has to be heated first then chilled whenever the system goes into a cycle.

Carp

Carp is similar to koi. They make good amounts of waste for the plants but nothing much else. Some ethnic restaurants do purchase carp. Best to check nearby markets before considering them for aquaponics.

Carnivorous fishes like bass, perch and crappies

These have a good demand for the market and fetch a pretty good price. However, fingerlings availability is limited and harvest is pretty restricted over a definite period.

Shrimp and Crayfish

These are detritivores, which feed on detritus or organic matter that tends to settle at the bottom of the tank. Some are also cannibalistic, meaning they also eat each other and pose some threats on the grower wanting to get a substantial yield. Some growers add them only to help clean the bottom of the tank.

Chapter 8: Aquaponics vs. Hydroponics

Hydroponics mainly deals with growing in a water medium. Aquaponics promotes nutrient cycles. The fish providing food for the plants through their waste and plants filters the water and makes it clean for the fishes.

Here are the other differences between aquaponics and hydroponics

- Nutrient supply

  In hydroponics, nutrients come from mixing chemical components into the water. In order for the plants to have constant nutrient supply, the nutrients have to be constantly added. This requires constant monitoring, adjusting and readjusting.

  This amount of work is not necessary with aquaponics. Nutrients are added into t he water naturally, through the fish waste and bacterial action. Fishes naturally waste and nitrification bacteria convert ammonia in the waste into nitrates and nitrites, which is food for the plants.

- Organic

  Hydroponics is less likely to produce organic plants. The constant addition of the chemicals into the water can be considered as a non-organic way of growing plants.

  In aquaponics, it's organic all the way. Plants depend on nutrients provided by fish waste and nothing else.

- Cost

  In hydroponics, chemicals need to be added into the water at regular intervals. The cost of these chemicals can add up the longer the hydroponics system operates. This is not an issue with aquaponics. The regular cost will mainly be on the fish feed.

- Yield

Growers attest that aquaponics produce more yield, with better quality and density compared to hydroponics. Harvest is larger and more abundant, in much less time than it takes with hydroponics.

Chapter 9: Tips And Tricks For A Successful Aquaponics Garden

For best results, there are a few things to consider when planning and setting up an aquaponics system.

Location

This is one of the first and most important things to consider when planning and setting up an aquaponics system. Make a survey of your home and backyard to see if which place is best. Consider space, sunlight, accessibility to electricity, ambient temperature, and exposure to winds and extremes in weather conditions. Make sure that the site is not within reach of pollution, toxin exposure and heavy foot traffic. Also, the setup should be away from chemicals not meant for aquaponics to avoid any poisoning accidents.

Water Oxygenation

Oxygen molecules in the atmosphere naturally dissolve into the water. Good water oxygenation is necessary for the fishes to thrive well. Plants in the hydroponics system help increase oxygen in the atmosphere. Aside from this, an air pump can help improve water oxygenation.

Water Additives

These may be necessary after the aquaponics system has been in operation for some time. At the beginning of the operation, fish waste can provide everything that the plants need. However, over time, as the plants grow, mature and start to bear flowers and fruits, their needs may be more than what the fishes can provide. Regularly check the water to check any element that may be lacking. Common additives would include calcium, iron and potassium.

Chapter 10: Caring Tips For Your Fish And Plants

The success of an aquaponics system depends on the success of the plants' and fishes' growth and reproduction. Aside from ensuring the right parameters such as temperature, oxygen and food levels, there are also a few things that growers need to give particular attention to.

Stocking fishes

In an aquaponics setup, you don't just throw any number of fish in the tank and hope for the best. Keeping a balance in the fish population is also necessary. While it is possible to stock as much fish as the tank can hold, experienced growers have something to say about this. Higher stocking densities have higher risks for things to go awfully wrong. It requires more work and attention because the grower has to make sure that all the parameters for maintaining an ideal water environment are at their ideal. More fishes mean that these parameters can abruptly change. Failing to address any change can lead to potential fish kill.

Seasoned growers recommend lowering the stocking densities to lower the stress, work and risk. High stocking densities is not an assurance of providing more food for the plants. In fact, plants still grow well and give sizeable yields even with a lightly stocked fish tank.

Placing the Plants

Where the plants are placed is also an important consideration. The level of the growing beds should be convenient for the grower and easy on the system. Place the plants too high and the pumps need to work harder in order to get the water from the fish tank to the beds. On the other hand, place the plants too low and your lower back will get strained from all the bending over you will be doing when tending to your plants.

Chapter 11: Shopping List For Starting Your Aquaponics Garden

Admittedly, a home aquaponics system, even if it is only small, requires quite a few supplies. The most essential ones include the following:

Bins

Bins are most important items in a setup. These house the fishes and the plants. Some gardeners use Rubbermaid tubs for their home aquaponics garden.

For fish bins, fish tanks or large Rubbermaid tubs can be used. Or, just about any container can be used to hold the fishes. Just make sure that the container can hold an adequate amount of water for the fishes to thrive in. Most fishes thrive better in relatively deeper water levels.

For the plants, shallow bins are more preferred. Plants tend to prefer aquatic habitats that do not hold too much water. It should be much shallower than bins used for fishes. The plant bin should be just deep enough for ample root support and shallow enough to allow a continuous water flow downwards to the bottom bins that hold the fishes.

Pumps

Pumps are important in an aquaponics system. These should be heavy duty because of the demands for their function.

Water pumps need to propel the water up from the fish tank and into the growing bin for the plants.

Air pumps are crucial in the fish bins. They add oxygen into the water, which the fishes are in most in need of. An air stone is often attached to the submerged end of the tube in order to create a lot of bubbles.

Timers are also necessary in order to regulate the water pumping between the tanks. An on/off cycle is necessary, which can be controlled by a timer. Typically, the pumps should work for 15 minutes, and then turned off for 45 minutes.

Hose

Hoses carry water up from the fish tank to the plant bins. Hoses may not seem much to look at, but their function is crucial. Growers should invest more on a solid and heavy duty hose when setting up a system.

Bird Wires or Fish Tank Covers

Well, fishes are delectable treats not just for humans but for other animals as well. Cats and birds are among the top predators that can get to the fishes. Protect them with covers such as bird wires.

Growing Medium

The growing medium is most important for the plants. These are placed in the pots where the plants are placed. Only the roots the plants should dangle down into the plant bins, where they absorb water. A popular growing medium is hydrogen balls. Other good media to use are perlite, pea stone and coconut fiber.

Water Test Kit

Water testing is important to determine and help maintain the crucial balance of nitrite and nitrate levels in the fish tank. The balance is very important in order for the fish to thrive and be healthy. Test the waters once per week to determine any need to adjust nitrite and nitrate levels.

Plants

Anything can be grown in an aquaponics system. This includes popular plants such as tomatoes, lettuce, peppers and strawberries.

Fishes

Fishes for the home aquaponics system can be raised for food purposes or as non edible pets. Tilapia is a very popular fish raised for food in home and backyard aquaponics. Koi can also be raised for non-food purposes.

Conclusion

Thank you again for purchasing this book on aquaponics.

I am extremely excited to pass this information along to you, and I am so happy that you now have read and can hopefully implement these strategies going forward.

I hope this book was able to help you understand aquaponics and how to set one up inn you home.

The next step is to get started using this information and to hopefully live a exciting life!

Please don't be someone who just reads this information and doesn't apply it, the strategies in this book will only benefit you if you use them!

If you know of anyone else that could benefit from the information presented here please inform them of this book.

Finally, if you enjoyed this book and feel it has added value to your life in any way, please take the time to share your thoughts and post a review on Amazon. It'd be greatly appreciated!

Thank you and good luck!

Preview Of:

<u>Fly Fishing</u>

A Fly Fishing Guide to Catching Trout Using Grandfather's Success Secrets For Fly Fishing!

Introduction

I want to thank you and congratulate you for purchasing the book, *"Fly Fishing: A Fly Fishing Guide To Catching Trout Using Grandfather's Success Secrets For Fly Fishing!"*

This book contains proven techniques and tricks to catching some world class trout.

I can still remember those trips that my Grandfather and I used to take. We knew the right spot, we had the right tackle, the right equipment, we knew the right strategies, and best of all we caught some seriously impressive trout!

I cherish those memories with Grandpa, and I know he did as well. It was a great time to get to know each other, and also to have some fun and catch the big ones.

My hope is that you can use this book filled with some killer techniques and tricks and not only create some fantastic memories, but also reel in some fish you'll be talking about for years to come.

Thanks again for purchasing this book, I hope you enjoy it!

Chapter 1: Know Your Fish

Trout fishing can be a fulfilling experience, whether you are doing it for fun, as a hobby, or even as a competitive sport. The fact that the fish can be found naturally in many parts of the world including North America, Asia, and Europe, and their generally tasty flesh make them desirable for many fishermen. Also, trout are known for giving a good fight when caught on a hook and line, and therefore they are sought-after as a good prize for recreational or competitive fishing.

While many people try to fish for trout, perhaps only a small percentage are truly able to master the art. Whether this is because of the number of years of experience under their belts, or the top-notch tactics and tricks that they keep up their sleeves, those successful in catching trout are truly looked up upon by other fishermen. It is hard to say just what it is that makes a man a successful trout catcher, but there are some basic tips and tricks that, although often taken for granted, can definitely turn anyone into a skillful fisher of trout.

The first thing that anyone who wishes to catch trout should know and understand is the fact that there are different types of trout, and that you should know your trout before you even try to think about catching them. The term trout is a very general name that is used to refer to a number of species of freshwater fish. Closely related to the salmon, these fish mostly live in freshwater lakes or rivers exclusively, but some are known to spend two to three years in the salty waters of the sea to spawn.

Knowing about the different types of trout does not necessarily mean that you should know all about the species and sub-species, but more so about their habitat and diet, and especially how they react to the different types of lures, baits, and fishing techniques that are used in trout fishing. Also of importance to trout catchers are the weight and sizes of the different types of trout as this can affect the outcome of any fishing endeavor.

Not all types of trout are ideal for the sport of trout fishing, but there are also those that stand out as being the most sought-after by trout fishermen. In most cases, it is also the location or wherever it is you are in the world that dictates the type of trout that you can go after. Here are some of the most popular types of trout that fishermen go after.

Rainbow Trout

The rainbow trout is among the most popular in the world of trout fishing. It is naturally found in many areas of the world namely the cold water regions of the Pacific Ocean in Asia and in North America. One of the distinguishing factors of this fish is the beautiful coloration from which it most likely got its name. While colors may vary depending on the fish's region of habitat, age, and spawning condition, most adult rainbow trout have a blue-green to olive green body with silvery sides. The body of the fish is also peppered with black spots, with some types being lined with a red band on the side. Others may have spots of reds and crimsons as well, making one think of watercolors on a canvas.

As for their size and weight, the rainbow trout grows in mass and weight as it lengthens or gets bigger in size. The average length of a rainbow trout is from 20 to 30 inches, with a weight of about 8 pounds. Depending on the fish's diet and habitat however, it can grow to as long as 4 feet and weigh as much as 53 pounds.

In terms of gaming, the rainbow trout is also one of the most sought-after because of the fight and challenge that it provides. The fish is known for leaping wildly about once it is hooked, and it can definitely put up a powerful fight because of its weight and agility. It is said that the fish can detect movements in the water from large distances, and that it can jump as high as four times its body length. Rainbow trout are considered to be among the top five sporting fish in North America, and is also the most popular in the Rocky Mountains region.

The popularity of the fish has prodded individuals to grow the Rainbow Trout in commercial fisheries, or even in regions where it is not part of the endemic wildlife. In Southern Europe, Australia, and South America, there has been much controversy because the introduction of the species to regions outside their own has caused negative effects on the local fish species. Rainbow trout have been known for preying on other native fish, for transmitting contagious diseases, and even for hybridizing with the local species, thus posing a threat to the native wildlife.

As a trivial fact, the world record for the Rainbow Trout as recognized by the International Game Fish Association was caught on September 5, 2009. The fish weighed in at 48 pounds, and it was discovered to have escaped from a genetically modified hatchery.

Brown Trout

The brown trout is another popular sporting fish for North American fishermen, but it is actually native to the waters of

Europe. It has been found to be a migrating species, thus it is found in different areas of the globe, though most are near the poles. This species is also easily recognizable by its brownish color that is dotted with pink or red spots on the sides and back.

Brown trout are considered to be medium-sized fish. A mature brown trout that lives in small rivers has an average weight of about 2 pounds, but in larger habitat, they can grow to as long as 55 inches and weigh as much as 60 pounds. As per records, the world's biggest trout ever to be caught was captured by a Mr. Tom Healy on September 11, 2009. The fish weighed in at 41.45 pounds, and it was found in the Manistee River system of Michigan.

Although native to Europe, the brown trout was introduced to North America, South America, New Zealand, Australia, and other countries where fishing enthusiasts lived. In most of these countries, the brown trout is a main focus for a specialized type of fishing known as fly fishing, and this has led to the artificial propagation of the species. As with the rainbow trout, the unnatural planting of the brown trout has posed threats to the native wildlife, and to the species itself.

This species of trout feeds mostly on a number of aquatic preys, most of which are invertebrates and water-dwelling insects. Compared with other species of trout, the brown trout is also known to be more predaceous as the large fish often feed at night on their unknowing prey.

When it comes to the fishing sport, brown trout are excellent targets for fly fishing because of their innate reliance on insect larvae and adult insects. Lures and baits that resemble these insects are often great for catching brown trout, and the fish is also known to spend long periods of time in one area of the river, unless they are spawning. Anglers should be aware however, that although the brown trout may seem relatively easy to lure, it is not quite easy to catch because of its predatory and more aggressive behavior.

The brown trout and the rainbow trout are only two species of trout, but they have other sub-species that can account for the majority of trout that are found in the different regions of the world. There are the steelhead trout, apache trout, golden trout, as well as the cutthroat trout. The main facts that a fisherman should consider are the way that each species behaves and just how big a challenge they can be. As with any sport, trout fishing requires that you know your targets first so that you may use the best of your abilities and what you have to catch them.

Thanks for Previewing My Exciting Book Entitled:

"Fly Fishing: A Fly Fishing Guide To Catching Trout Using Grandfather's Success Secrets For Fly Fishing!"

To purchase this book, simply go to the Amazon Kindle store and simply search:

"FLY FISHING"

Then just scroll down until you see my book. You will know it is mine because you will see my name "David Wright" underneath the title.

Alternatively, you can visit my author page on Amazon to see this book and other work I have done. Thanks so much, and please don't forget your free bonuses

DON'T LEAVE YET! - CHECK OUT YOUR FREE BONUSES BELOW!

Free Bonus Offer: Get Free Access To The www.LuxyLifeNaturals.com VIP Newsletter!

Once you enter your email address you will immediately get free access to this awesome newsletter!

But wait, right now if you join now for free you will also get free access to the "Secrets of Becoming A Meditation Expert – In 7 Days!" free Ebook!

To claim both your FREE VIP NEWSLETTER MEMBERSHIP and your FREE BONUS Ebook on the SECRETS OF BECOMING A MEDITATION EXPERT IN 7 DAYS!

Just Go To:

www.LuxyLifeNaturals.com

www.ingramcontent.com/pod-product-compliance
Lightning Source LLC
Chambersburg PA
CBHW061933280526
45787CB00004B/1589